Uncommon Sense

Uncommon Sense

How to Think Clearly When the World Has Lost Its Mind

Jack Valerio

Valerio Publishing

This book was developed with the assistance of artificial intelligence as a collaborative tool. The ideas, voice, and final expression belong to the human author.

Published by Valerio Publishing

ISBN: 979-8-9942573-0-2

First Edition
Printed in the United States of America

Table of Contents

Acknowledgments vii
Preface ix

Section I
The Cost of Excellence

1. The Toll Booth at the Edge of Average 3
2. You're Not Bad at It—You're Just Committed to Failing! 5
3. Stopping Short of Excellence 8
4. The Willing Few 11

Section II
Seeing What We Usually Miss

5. The Worst Ideas Are The Ones We Don't Question 17
6. What We Think We Know—But Don't 20
7. The Second Opinion Is Yours 24
8. Stop Blaming Roosters 27
9. You're Never the Smartest One in the Room 30

Section III
Why Smart People Stay Stuck

10. When Everyone Nods in Agreement 35
11. Don't Learn from the Best 38
12. Read Tomorrow's Newspaper Today 41
13. The Future Isn't Asking for Your Agreement 44
14. What's Stopping You? 47
15. You're Not Stuck—You're Just Thinking Like Everybody Else 49

Section IV
How Influence Really Works

16. Stop Telling—Do This Instead 55
17. Stop Expecting People to Do What They're Supposed to Do 58
18. The Most Loving Thing You Can Do 61
19. How to Push a Mule Up a Hill 64

Section V
Recalibrating the Inner Scale

20. You Hold the Scale 71
21. The Day You Put the Tools Away 75
22. Don't Let the Rain Blind You 78
23. Why We Need to Understand People from Another Galaxy 81

A Note To Readers 85
Afterword 86

Acknowledgments

I am deeply grateful to the people who walked this path with me, especially the woman who read every chapter and helped me hear my own words, and to the tool that helped me finally begin. This book is also a quiet thank-you to my parents, my family, my students, my friends, and everyone who shaped the way I think.

For forty-two years I worked as an educator, spending my days with young people. Being with students every day forced me to keep changing how I think, how I listen, and how I see the world. Just when I would begin to understand one group of students, a new group would arrive with a completely different way of seeing things, and I had to adjust all over again. Watching the world arrive in new forms, year after year, trained me to expect change and stay open to it. The way I look at people and problems in this book comes directly from that experience.

This book was not written in isolation. It was written with the constant presence of a real reader. My girlfriend lived inside the chapters as they were being born and as they grew into what they eventually became. She represented the reader to whom I was writing. I always knew what I was trying to say, but I did not always know what a reader would think or feel when I said it. Her reactions, questions, and moments of clarity or confusion showed me what my words were actually doing inside another human being. Because she stood in for every reader, her voice shaped this book in ways I could never have done alone.

I owe more than I can ever express to my parents. They built my self-image long before the world had a chance to damage it. I was never belittled, never made to feel small, and never left to doubt my worth. From them I learned dignity, fairness, and what it means to care deeply about other people. My father showed me humanity through action, and my mother taught me love through devotion. Together they gave me a foundation of confidence and values that I have carried into every part of my life.

The struggles we all face in life have been some of my greatest teachers. While I was always a serious learner, I did not shine as a student, and I often found myself behind others academically. What mattered more than grades was that every time I proved to myself that I could do the work, a quiet confidence was built that never left me. Life later brought other serious challenges, including some life-threatening illnesses and deeply difficult emotional moments. I refused to allow those circumstances to break me. Instead, I allowed them to shape me. I learned to work through them rather than surrender to them, and that mindset has followed me throughout my life.

For years people told me I should write a book and I always brushed it off. One day I was talking with ChatGPT, an artificial intelligence app, about an idea it felt had value for others, and it said, "You should write a book, and I'm ready to help you." That simple exchange finally made me believe this book could be written.

This book matters to me because I am an educator who no longer works inside a traditional classroom. What I have now is a way of sharing how I see the world with anyone who chooses to read these pages. Through a lifetime of personal struggle and relentless learning, I have developed a habit of noticing patterns, thinking deeply about problems, and seeing possibilities that others often overlook. I do not want that understanding to end with me. I want it to be passed along, to reach beyond the people I can touch directly and even beyond my own lifetime. This book is my way of giving that understanding to others while I still can.

Preface

This is not a book of clever ideas. It is a book shaped by experience.

Everything in these pages grew out of a lifetime of watching how people think, decide, and act in the real world — not in theory, and not only in classrooms, but in families, friendships, workplaces, schools, and communities, in moments where decisions mattered and consequences followed. Those experiences came from my own childhood and education, from raising children, building relationships, following passions, working different jobs, living in different places, and spending decades inside and outside professional environments. Taken together, they taught me how things actually work.

This book is about seeing.

Seeing situations differently.

Seeing assumptions clearly.

Seeing options that are too frequently missed.

Seeing what is really there, rather than what we are used to seeing.

Most people are not held back by a lack of intelligence. They are held back by habits of thought that go unquestioned. Many of the ideas we casually call "common sense" are popular, familiar, and widely accepted, but that does not make them correct. Some are incomplete. Others are counterproductive. Still others are simply wrong. When something is genuinely effective, practical, and grounded in reality, it is often uncommon. That is why I call what this book offers uncommon sense.

Over time, my work as an educator taught me something simple but essential about how people actually come to understand new ideas. Telling someone what to think rarely works. What works far better is asking questions, allowing space for reflection, and giving people the chance to see things for themselves. When that happens, the conclusions they reach are not imposed. They are owned.

That is how this book is written.

Section I

The Cost of Excellence

Chapter One

The Toll Booth at the Edge of Average

People often ask me to recommend a good doctor. When I name one, the next question is almost always, "Where is he located?" If I say thirty minutes away, they groan: "That's far!" My reply is simple: "Do you want good, or do you want close?"

That groan says more than people realize. People say they want the best care, but even a short drive is enough to stop most of them. The distance isn't unreasonable. The inconvenience just feels like too high a price to pay for what they claim to want.

I saw the same pattern in education. When I decided to pursue school administration, I enrolled in graduate school while still teaching full-time. Colleagues who already held administrative degrees reacted with disbelief. The system was rigged, they said. Connections mattered more than competence. Applying was a waste of time.

When I finished the degree, the doubts didn't disappear — they shifted. People told me not to bother applying, that decisions were made long before interviews ever happened. Many had tried a few times, failed, and stopped. Convinced the outcome was predetermined, they quit early and explained their exit as realism.

I went to interviews knowing I probably wouldn't be chosen. What others never even considered was that effort can still separate candidates, even when outcomes feel fixed. Most showed up having done the minimum. I prepared as if preparation mattered — because sometimes it does, and when it does, it matters a lot.

At twenty-seven, I became an assistant principal. Not because of special connections or luck, but because I kept doing what others had already decided wasn't worth the effort. Persistence didn't guarantee success, but quitting guaranteed failure.

For me, "unable" never meant "impossible." As a full-time teacher, I still found ways to visit schools — sometimes by using personal days, other times by giving up a day's pay. The cost wasn't trivial, but it drew a clear line between wanting something and being willing to earn it.

Years later, I encountered the same toll booth in a different setting. While planning a new dance event, I spent over two months building a database, advertising across social media groups, and following up with emails and texts. The work was deliberate and time-consuming, and it all happened before the first song was ever played.

Before the event ever happened, I spoke with a woman who was a regular attendee at several local dance venues. When I mentioned hosting my event on Sunday afternoons instead of evenings, she dismissed the idea outright: "Nobody will come."

She couldn't see the work behind the decision. She couldn't see that the toll had already been paid. When more than eighty people showed up — far more than at any local studio dance — the result seemed surprising to her. It wasn't. It was earned.

Across careers, decades, and circumstances, the pattern never changed. Whether it's avoiding a thirty-minute drive, quitting after a few rejections, skipping preparation, or clinging to what feels comfortable, people stop at the same place. Not because the goal is unreachable, but because the price feels inconvenient.

I once saw a sign on a classroom ceiling that said, "If you want to achieve what others don't, you have to do what others won't."

That sign points to the toll booth — the place at the edge of average that guards the bridge to excellence. The toll is rarely money. It's effort, sacrifice, persistence, and discipline. Those willing to pay it move forward. Those who aren't stay where they are, still wanting what lies beyond, but rarely reaching it.

Chapter Two

You're Not Bad at It—You're Just Committed to Failing!

All my life, people told me, "You can do it." I believed them then, and I believe them now. But those words alone never seemed enough.

Here's the uncomfortable truth: most people aren't bad at something because they lack ability. They're bad at it because, somewhere along the way, they gave themselves permission to fail. They didn't lack talent. They lacked the confidence to commit. For example, some say, "I'll try," instead of deciding they're going to do it. That small difference matters. Leaving yourself that out almost guarantees a half-hearted attempt. When that attempt falls short, it starts to feel like proof that you're not good at it, reinforcing the belief that you never were.

Over time, a downward spiral can occur. When you keep telling yourself you're not good at something, you stop putting in real effort. With less effort, you don't improve. When you don't improve, your confidence drops. And when your confidence drops, you become even less willing to try the next time.

Fortunately, the same mechanism can work in the opposite direction. When you tell yourself you can improve, you put in real effort. With real effort, you get better. As you get better, your confidence grows. And when your confidence grows, you become more willing to keep going. The same cycle can carry you toward improvement or quietly drag you toward failure. Which way it runs depends on what you tell yourself at the start.

By the time I was 47, I believed I had a clear map of what I could and couldn't do. Dancing wasn't just off that map. It felt like it belonged somewhere else entirely. I simply believed it was impossible. That belief matched the way others already saw me. When it came to dancing, I was the person sitting at a table, not the one on the floor.

Around that same time, my wife and I separated. She was a Puerto

Rican woman, and her warmth, affection, and emotional openness felt immediately familiar to me. I grew up in Italian and Jewish worlds where closeness and expressiveness mattered, and her culture fit naturally with that. Latin music and salsa were central to who she was, and they were things I had been surrounded by long before our marriage. My brother played Latin music constantly when I was growing up, and I absorbed it without ever thinking about it. So when I imagined finding that same depth and intensity again, I knew it would be within that same cultural world.

I didn't live in a Latin community, and my most direct access to that world was through Latin clubs and events. And Latin clubs are not places where you sit at a table. They are places where you dance. Which meant that if I wanted what I was after, I had to undo the belief that I couldn't dance. Learning wasn't optional. Quitting wasn't an option either. The decision had already been made.

So I went. I was anxious, but completely determined. The first night, I danced once and left as quickly as though I were escaping a crime scene. It didn't deter me. I went back. Eventually, I took lessons.

And then something happened. One day my instructor asked me to lead her into a turn. I did, and she turned. I didn't say a word. But on the drive home, alone in the car, I cried, and through the tears I said out loud, "I can do this." In that moment, a belief I had carried for decades collapsed. I wasn't incapable. I had simply been convinced that I was. Once that conviction broke, it never came back. Dance became my passion, not because I was born for it, but because I refused to keep believing a lie.

When I first moved into my 55-plus community, I had little interest in organized activities. I chose the location because it put me close to dance events almost every night of the week. That was my world. But Mondays were empty in the dance scene, and eventually I wandered into the clubhouse and discovered karaoke night.

For weeks, I stayed silent in the crowd. I had no intention of singing. My mind kept running back to junior high school, when a music teacher confirmed what I already feared: I couldn't sing. That moment stayed with me for decades. But after several weeks of listening, something shifted. A familiar inner voice spoke up: "I think I can do this." It wasn't arrogance. I had heard that voice before, and I knew what it meant. Still, I wasn't completely convinced.

So I consulted people I trusted. My best friend had no doubts. My daughter, who had been paid to sing professionally, agreed. My girlfriend did as well. Eventually, I tested it privately. I sang for her. She was convinced. One night, instead of sitting and listening, I signed up. I've been singing ever since, and I keep getting better.

That story isn't about singing any more than the earlier one was about dancing. They're simply two expressions of the same truth. Confidence doesn't usually follow competence. It comes before it. When confidence and commitment are in place, limits lose their power to hold us back. What once felt impossible becomes routine. What once brought discomfort becomes joy, not because talent suddenly appears, but because belief stops working against you.

Most people aren't held back by a lack of ability. They're held back by beliefs they've rehearsed for years without realizing it, beliefs that say it's too late, that they're not wired for this, that failure is inevitable. Those beliefs feel factual. They aren't!

Confidence isn't blind optimism. It's a grounded conviction built from decision and follow-through. It grows when you stop defending your doubts and start acting as if success is mandatory.

At some point, you have to stop rehearsing your limitations. Achievement doesn't wait for talent. It waits for commitment.

Chapter Three

Stopping Short of Excellence

Most people don't stop short because they lack talent. They stop because they think they've already done enough. "Good enough" feels safe, and when success looks final, they call it done. The hard part isn't reaching excellence — it's realizing that "good enough" isn't it. Some stop because they believe they've already arrived. Others stop because they assume excellence lies somewhere beyond their reach. Either way, they settle where it feels comfortable and stay there.

There's a moment just beyond that point — a moment people often sense and then turn away from. You feel it when a quiet question appears: *Could this be better?* It's the instant when curiosity replaces comfort, when something inside you suggests you're not quite finished. It's easy to ignore. Not everyone does.

When I became a DJ, my goal wasn't to build the biggest playlist — it was to build the best. Every track had to earn its place. I wasn't interested in "good enough." To make that happen, I danced to every song first. If it didn't make my body move or touch something deeper, I deleted it immediately. I didn't even want it sitting on my computer. I also asked a trusted friend trained in fifteen different dances to listen to each one. If she didn't respond with genuine enthusiasm or describe it as exceptional, it was deleted. It wasn't hard work; it simply required care and attention. That small difference changed everything. Over time, the result was a collection made up only of music that met a clear standard — and when I played, the nights reflected that. There was nothing in the mix to pull the energy down or make it feel ordinary.

Years earlier, the same questions showed up in a very different setting. In my last position in education as an assistant principal, I revised the student and teacher handbooks every year, line by line. I could have reissued the old versions, as many schools did, or made a few changes alone and moved on. Instead, I took one more step. I photocopied the relevant sections and sent them to the people who lived them every day — the principal, assistant principals, the athletic director, teachers, and support staff — and asked for their input. When their notes came back, I refined and clarified each section until the handbooks reflected not just policy, but real understanding and care.

At home, the questions were quieter, but they were the same. Whenever I cook, I watch closely as the first bites are taken, waiting for the reaction. If I hear, "This is excellent," or "This is really good," that's gratifying — but I don't stop there. I taste it myself, and if something feels just slightly off, I notice. I start asking questions: Could the flavors run deeper? Could the texture soften? Is one note overpowering the others? I try to lift what's already good until it feels complete. It isn't perfectionism that drives me, but joy — the satisfaction of knowing that what's shared at the table couldn't be any better in that moment.

You see the same thing in small, ordinary places if you're paying attention. A waiter refills your glass before you ask. A cashier double-bags your groceries when it's raining so they won't tear on the way to your car. An employee doesn't let the conversation end when you're uncertain but offers one more idea that might actually help. These aren't grand gestures. They're small acts of awareness and care — choices people make when they decide not to stop at what's required. Excellence isn't limited to major accomplishments or impressive titles. It shows up quietly, in moments where no one would notice if you didn't bother.

Most people stop at "good enough," do what's expected, and move on. A few don't. They give a little more of themselves, not because they have to, but because they notice when something is still unfinished. Over time, that habit shapes not only what they do, but who they become. Excellence isn't a giant leap. It's the decision not to stop. It's listening when that inner voice suggests there might be something more, and choosing to respond. That final ten percent is what separates the ordinary from the remarkable — the space between saying, "That'll do," and asking, "What else can I do?"

Excellence has nothing to do with perfection. It's about pride — the quiet kind that comes from caring enough to do something well. It's about respect — for your work, for the people it touches, and for yourself. You don't have to chase excellence in everything you do. Life doesn't demand that. But if "good enough" has become your default, it's worth changing in at least one place. Choose a part of your life — your craft, your teaching, your cooking, your work, your relationships — and refuse to settle there. Give a little more, and notice how close excellence has always been.

Most people never realize how close it is. It isn't far away; it begins just beyond the point where you think you're finished. The distance between average and extraordinary is rarely more than ten percent. That voice inside you — the one that doesn't quite let things go — isn't doubt. It's wisdom. It's the part of you that still sees what's possible when the rest of you wants to stop. Don't silence it. Listen to it. Let it lead you past the comfort of "good enough." Each time you do, you move closer to mastery — to a pride that needs no applause, and to a life where you take the time to do things right instead of just getting them done.

Chapter Four

The Willing Few

I used to live in a 55-plus community in St. Cloud, Florida. The neighborhood was new and still growing, which meant a steady stream of people who had just moved in and were still figuring things out. Questions came up constantly, especially about local services. One question came up again and again. It always sounded simple: “Can you recommend a doctor?”

My answer was always the same: “Yes, absolutely.” I’d tell them about a doctor I trusted and explain why, what kind of physician he was, what set him apart, and why I felt comfortable recommending him. Almost without exception, the follow-up question came immediately: “Where is he located?” And when I answered, the response was just as predictable: “That’s far!”

It didn’t take long to realize that the important part of that exchange wasn’t the recommendation itself. It was the response to it. People said they were looking for the best, but that turned out not to be entirely true. The moment they learned that getting the best required some inconvenience, they were no longer interested. In this case, distance was the dividing line. Any degree of extra effort on their part was the deal-breaker. What initially sounded like a question about quality turned out to be something completely different: How much quality can I get without any real cost to me?

I used to go dancing at a local restaurant that offered free dancing if you met a minimum purchase requirement. The draw for me was the music and the dance floor rather than the food. I wasn’t there to eat, but a purchase was required, so each time I went I ordered an appetizer just to clear that bar, and it was almost always the same one.

The dish was a fairly good eggplant rollatini with nothing much wrong with it. However, after having it a few times, I began to notice that I was paying much more attention to what was missing than what was present. It wasn't a memorable meal as it was presented. There was no depth to it. It didn't make me want another bite after the first. It was food that did its job in a minimal way and stopped there.

I couldn't stop thinking about how the dish might become memorable instead of merely satisfactory. So I went home and did a little research—nothing elaborate. I wasn't trying to reinvent the dish. I made a few minor changes, one of which was using my own sauce instead of the one the restaurant used. When I made it that way, the improvement was clear. The dish was better.

When I served it to my then girlfriend, she agreed. For her, that was enough. The dish was better, and the problem had been solved. There was no reason to keep working on it. I didn't see it that way, not because it wasn't good, but because it still wasn't memorable. I could tell there was more there if I was willing to keep working on it. When I said it was good but not quite there yet, she was genuinely surprised. In her mind, the stopping point had already been reached.

The difference between us was in our level of willingness. For many people, the moment a result becomes acceptable, that's the moment the effort ends. "Good enough" becomes the signal to stop. A smaller number are willing to keep working on it, not because something is broken, but because something can still be easily improved.

New Yorkers who move to Florida all talk about the same thing. They say they're looking for real New York–style pizza. They mean it, or at least it seems that way. They try one place, maybe two. If the pizza is decent, they settle. They declare it the best around and stop looking, not because it really is, but because continuing the search would take more time, more effort, and maybe a longer drive.

Later, when I mentioned to friends that I had finally found a place that made great New York–style pizza, none of them had heard of it. That wasn't because the place was hidden. It was because they had stopped earlier. They didn't stop because they couldn't find better. They stopped because finding better would have required time and effort they weren't willing to put in. Once they stopped, whatever they had found became "the best" in their minds.

None of these situations required exceptional intelligence, access, or luck. They simply required willingness — the willingness to do that little bit extra most people won't do. To try one more time. To go a little farther. To keep working on something even after it already works. That little bit extra is where the willing few separate themselves from everyone else.

Section II

Seeing What We Usually Miss

Chapter Five

The Worst Ideas Are The Ones We Don't Question

We live in a world drowning in information but starving for clarity. And if you're honest, you already know that more information hasn't made you wiser—it's just made it easier to stop thinking. The real explain-away isn't that life is too complicated. It's that we keep mistaking common knowledge for truth. And once you accept something as "everyone knows this," you stop examining it. You stop testing it. You stop noticing when it quietly fails you.

You've heard things like, "Breakfast is the most important meal of the day." Or, "Humans only use ten percent of their brain." Or, "Sugar makes kids hyper." They sound right. They feel familiar. They've been repeated so often they barely register as claims anymore—they feel like facts. They're not. They're wrong. And if you've accepted even one of them without ever checking it, then you've already seen how common knowledge works on you.

People rely on ideas like these every day, not because they're true, but because repetition makes them feel true. Once enough people repeat something, questioning it starts to feel unnecessary—even impolite. That's how common knowledge gains its power: not through evidence, but through agreement.

My own rule has always been simple: never follow blindly, never accept thoughtlessly, and never confuse familiarity with truth. If something doesn't quite ring true, that's not a flaw—that's a signal.

Take the old saying, "Practice makes perfect." It sounds harmless. Encouraging, even. Most people nod along without hesitation. But it's wrong. Practice doesn't make perfect. Only correct practice does. Practice the wrong way, and you don't improve—you lock in your mistakes. You don't get better. You just get more consistent at doing the wrong thing.

Nowhere is this clearer than in something you probably believe you already do well: driving. Most people get a license at sixteen and assume that years behind the wheel automatically translate into skill. By the time they're thirty-six, they're still driving like sixteen-year-olds—just with twenty years of bad habits layered on top. Why? Because the license, which should be permission to learn, is treated like a lifetime certificate of competence. It shouldn't be. A license should mark the beginning, not the end. A year of supervised driving. Then a real test—not just of rules, but of awareness, control, judgment, and precision. None of that happens now, and you can see the results every day on the road.

I didn't learn to drive at sixteen. I grew up in New York City. No car. No need. While suburban teenagers were counting down birthdays, I was riding subways and buses. In the city, licenses came later, driver's education was uncommon, and owning a car wasn't automatic. For me, it made sense to wait until I was twenty-one—until I actually needed to drive. When I finally did learn, I took it seriously. I read. I studied technique. I practiced with intention. And that's when something became obvious: most people don't drive well. They just drive often.

They drift over lane lines. Block intersections. Roll through stop signs. Treat speed limits as casual suggestions. And because no one ever forces them to improve, they never do. Years pass. Habits harden. Confidence rises. Skill doesn't. That's the trap of common knowledge: repetition masquerading as mastery. Time gets mistaken for competence. Familiarity replaces judgment.

And this pattern doesn't stop with driving. You see it in health myths too. "Salt causes high blood pressure" is repeated so often it feels settled. But it's only half true. Salt doesn't cause hypertension. It worsens it in people who already have the condition. That distinction matters—because confusing correlation with cause leads to bad decisions. Believing otherwise is like thinking umbrellas cause rain simply because you see them together.

The real danger isn't bad information. You can spot that easily. The danger is accepting information without resistance. Once you stop questioning, you start letting others do your thinking. You act on ideas you've never tested. You defend beliefs you never chose. And that's how people end up confident, consistent, and wrong.

The moment you stop questioning, you hand over control—not dramatically, but quietly. You follow paths that don't lead where you expect. You make decisions that feel reasonable and still fail you. And you never quite understand why.

The worst ideas aren't the outrageous ones. Those are easy to reject. The worst ideas are the ones you never pause to question—the ones everyone accepts without thinking. So the next time you hear something presented as common knowledge, don't nod. Pause. Ask yourself whether it's actually true, or whether it's just been repeated long enough to feel that way. Because once you stop questioning, you stop choosing. And that's a habit with consequences.

Chapter Six
What We Think We Know—But Don't

Everyone is entitled to an informed opinion, one grounded in fact. But an uninformed opinion is just a conclusion made without knowledge or understanding, usually drawn from assumptions or limited experience. And a perfect example of this kind of uninformed conclusion is the way people think they understand education.

There's a curious phenomenon in education that you don't see in many other lines of work. Most people assume they understand the profession simply because they went through school themselves.

No one thinks they're a surgeon because they've visited a hospital. Very few people believe they understand the law just because they once sat in a courtroom. But when it comes to education, especially K–12, many suddenly see themselves as experts, ready to judge, correct, and even tell teachers how to do their jobs. And it all comes from one thing, their experience in school as children.

So how did so many people come to believe they understand schools and teaching when they don't? The answer is simple. You went to school, so naturally you assume you understand how it works.

When you attended elementary and secondary school, you had the mind of a child, not the insight of a mature adult. You were close enough to see what schools and teachers were doing, but you were not always equipped to understand what much of it actually meant. What you saw was filtered through a child's brain, not one that could yet make complete sense of why adults were doing what they were doing.

That illusion has been reinforced for years by movies, television, and political rhetoric. And let's be honest, you have likely never spent a full day in a school since developing your adult eyes, ears, and mind.

The mistaken belief that you understand what really happens in schools often gets reinforced rather than corrected. You hear other adults in the community talk about school, many of them carrying the same misperceptions you formed from your own childhood experience, and you hear your own children describe what happens in their classrooms even though they do not yet have the perspective to fully understand their own school experience. Put it all together, and your picture of what is happening inside schools is not just incomplete. It is a distortion of reality.

I spent more than four decades in education, teaching, leading, mentoring teachers, and helping shape school and district policy. And in all that time I encountered more people than I can count who assumed they knew better, not because they had studied teaching or spent time in classrooms as professionals, but simply because they once went to school as children, took a few tests, ate lunch in the cafeteria, and played in the schoolyard.

Over the years I learned that some of the most unnecessarily difficult moments in education come from conversations with parents who walk in already convinced they understand what happened, what it means, and how it should be handled. Their concern is not the problem. Parents should come in with beliefs, doubts, and real questions about their child.

The problem is how those beliefs are brought into the room. Instead of approaching the conversation with inquiry, the way you would with a doctor or any other professional, being convinced turns the exchange into accusation and conclusion. What should have been a conversation about a child becomes a challenge to the people whose job it is to understand that child best.

There are many reasons teachers deserve to be treated as professionals, and one of the biggest is how much training they actually go through. The overwhelming majority eventually earn master's degrees, and in many districts that degree is also the standard path to higher pay for doing the same job. In other words, teachers don't just go back to school because they're told to. The profession is built to value and reward continued education. On top of that, teachers are often required to return to universities for additional coursework outside of the master's degree. If a school decides that teachers need training in something like English as a second language because of the students they serve, then teachers are expected to go out and get that training no matter how many degrees they already hold. And then there is in-service training, the ongoing, job-related learning that continues throughout a teacher's entire career. For many educators, that adds up to decades of continuous training, a level of professional development few other professions ever demand.

Every profession is made up of two parts, what you learn in training and what you learn by doing the work. Teaching is not a scripted job. Teachers plan, but everyday reality forces constant unanticipated changes. Students may be bored, confused, distracted, upset, or struggling, sometimes all during the same instructional period. In those moments, teachers do not have the privilege of pressing a pause button so they can think. They have to think on their feet, adjust their approach, and make decisions in real time in front of a room full of children. That does not happen once in a while. It happens every day throughout an entire career. And it is that repeated, lived experience, not just degrees on the wall, that qualifies teachers as professionals.

Schools are the most powerful tool a society has for shaping its future, and teachers are the professionals trained to make that tool work. That is why how you treat educators matters so much. But underestimating the professionalism of teachers is only part of the problem. The other part is when you act on the false assumption that you already understand how schools work and what teachers do. Those two attitudes combine in ways that do not serve the needs of children. They turn what should be collaboration into opposition and create an adversarial posture that is unnecessary, unproductive, and harmful to the very child you are trying to help.

Teachers are not looking to be celebrated. They're not interested in apples on their desks or certificates on Teacher Appreciation Day. They expect you to walk into school the same way you walk into any other professional setting, with questions rather than conclusions, with curiosity instead of declarations, and with a willingness to learn rather than a closed-mind approach.

They want a cooperative relationship with families, not an adversarial one. They want the same thing you want for your children, for them to be as prepared as possible for the adult world that awaits them, and they know that happens best when they work together with you. So don't come armed with certainty. Come prepared to listen, to ask, and to learn. That's partnership.

The next time you walk into your child's school with a problem, a concern, or even just a question, remember the title of this chapter, *What We Think We Know — But Don't*. Pause long enough to listen, to ask, and to learn. Because when you do, you make it possible for teachers to work with you, and for you to work with them, as true partners in the one mission that matters more than anything else, your child's success.

Chapter Seven

The Second Opinion Is Yours

Not long ago, I received a text from a friend—an accomplished author—to whom I had emailed early drafts of the first few chapters of my book. Instead of commenting on the content, she wisely began by asking about my purpose. Was I planning to publish it, or simply share it with friends and family? I told her, tongue-in-cheek, that I was aiming big—New York Times bestseller-list big. I was writing not just for my inner circle, but for anyone who might benefit from the uncommon wisdom I've spent a lifetime gathering.

Her response was brief: "Some publishers won't publish AI books. Look into it." I took it seriously because I knew it wasn't meant to discourage me. Most advice isn't. It's usually meant to protect people from embarrassment or failure, and the people who give it often care deeply about you. In her case, she was sharing what she believed was the reality of the publishing world.

The words themselves were fine, but the sentence felt like a stop sign. To her, it was probably a yellow light—a reminder to be cautious. To me, it was a red one I refused to obey. I wasn't going to let myself be stopped by the idea that large numbers of publishers might not want an AI-assisted book.

I texted back, "That's their problem," because I believe a great book should stand or fall on its own merit, not on the method used to create it. Whether it's typed on an old IBM Selectric typewriter or spoken into a voice-to-text app, brilliance is brilliance, quality is quality, and excellence is excellence.

The world is always giving us chances to weigh advice, usually from caring people who believe they're helping. I had one of those moments when I told two local dancers I was planning a new Sunday-afternoon social dance in Stuart, Florida.

For years, they'd gone to another studio's dance on that same day, and this new idea felt like a replacement, not an addition. They pushed back immediately. Their advice came as warnings: "Sunday's a tough day," and "Nobody will come."

I listened carefully. They weren't wrong to worry, but their experience came from a small studio with a handful of regulars—that was the world they knew. My plan was different. I wasn't building for one room of familiar faces, but for hundreds of dancers across the region, in an elegant, centrally located venue just two minutes from the highway and easy to reach for both locals and people who live in nearby towns. So I did what I've learned to do when advice collides with reality: I listened, I weighed it, and then I decided for myself.

At my age it's normal to see more than one doctor, and I do—a primary care physician and a few specialists, all carefully chosen and deeply trusted. The visits are thorough. They ask good questions, listen, give me the chance to ask mine, explain what they're doing, and then the appointment ends with their conclusion.

It's often only later, walking to the car, that the doubts show up. Why didn't I ask that? Why didn't we review my medications? The diplomas on the wall, the white coat, the years of training all send the same message: they know, you don't. So we nod, thank them, and leave carrying statements we never made and questions we never asked.

For me, the most important issue is my kidney disease. It isn't a major problem right now, but it could become one if my kidney function declined even slightly. That's why I pay close attention to medications I've taken for years that are processed by the kidneys. No one has ever sat down with me and said, "Let's review every medication you're taking—not just the ones I prescribed—to see how they affect your kidneys and whether a change in medication or dosage is possible." So I learned to do it myself. For each medication I now ask, *Can the dosage be reduced and still work? Is there a newer drug that provides the same benefit but doesn't get processed by the kidneys? And is the benefit of continuing to take this drug still worth the potential cost?*

Sometimes nothing changes. The medication stays the same. The plan stays the same. The doctor remains confident and professional, but the shift isn't in the chart—it's in the room. When the second opinion is yours, you're no longer just hearing conclusions; you're helping shape them. That's the difference between being informed and being responsible. Simply following the advice of others is being informed. Deciding whether that advice applies to you in whole, in part, or not at all—that's being responsible.

Advice can be kind, expert, even loving. It can also be self-protective, motivated by fear, or quietly serving someone else's interests rather than yours. But motive is a distraction. What matters is that a second opinion is essential—and that second opinion has to be yours.

Don't walk away carrying decisions that others made for you. Stop, think, and decide what's best for you. Advice should inform you, not control you. Your life shouldn't be shaped by what you were told. It should be shaped by what you ultimately chose after you heard what others had to say.

The second and final opinion is yours.

Chapter Eight

Stop Blaming Roosters

The classic example of bad reasoning goes back centuries. The rooster crows, and shortly afterward the sun rises. It happens day after day. One thing appears before another, but does that mean the first caused the second?

The truth is that the rooster's crow and the sunrise have nothing to do with each other. The rooster isn't responsible for the sun coming up. Yet for a long time, people believed otherwise. It's easy to understand why. When one thing follows another consistently, the mind starts to connect them. It feels like logic because it looks like logic, but it isn't logic at all.

We may not blame roosters for the sun rising anymore, but we make the same kind of mistake every day. A driver successfully weaves through traffic and concludes he's a great driver. In reality, the only reason he isn't in a wreck is because everyone around him is a good driver who slows down and makes room for him. They avoid the accidents he would otherwise cause. When someone starts taking a supplement, notices he's getting sick less often, and concludes the supplement is the reason, even though scientific evidence directly contradicts that belief. These are today's roosters, the false beliefs that allow us to conclude a cause-and-effect relationship exists when it actually doesn't.

These examples rest on the same false notion, that two things occurring close together means one must have caused the other. It's a comfortable way to explain the world, especially when we want credit for a positive outcome or need a reason for something that didn't go our way. It allows us to create neat stories to explain a world that rarely fits together as neatly as we'd like.

Even major institutions fall into this trap. What happened to me as a young man working my way through college is a perfect example of how ludicrous this kind of thinking can become. I worked as a summer teller at a bank, full-time during the summers and part-time on holidays throughout the year. I had worked at several branches of the same bank and was always considered a strong asset. My reviews were positive. Customers responded well. In every location, the staff and managers were pleased with my work.

One summer I was assigned to a new branch. I met another teller there, and we began having regular conversations. Over time, it became clear that she had difficulty accepting opinions that differed from her own, and at times she became loud and openly angry. Eventually, I decided that the best course was to distance myself from her, but the damage had already been done. She remained bothered by those conversations and ultimately decided to complain about me to the branch manager.

Shortly after that, I met with the branch manager at his request. He didn't ask me to explain my side of the story or invite me to tell it. Instead, he said the branch had been functioning smoothly before I arrived and that, since my arrival, there was now a conflict between me and another teller. From that, he concluded that I had to be the cause. On the basis of that false logic, he sent me downtown to personnel.

The person in personnel listened to my story in full and recommended a voluntary reassignment. I accepted, but I also objected to the reason behind my being sent downtown, that the branch manager had assumed cause and effect simply because one thing followed another. There were no other facts that supported that conclusion. He had confused coincidence with responsibility for what occurred. In short, he blamed the rooster for the sunrise.

When one thing happens and another follows, the mind is quick to connect them. Too often, we conclude that the first caused the second. Sometimes that's true, but often it isn't.

Every time you make that mistake, it carries a potential cost. It may damage your reputation. It may leave you wrong in situations where being right is of the utmost importance. It may lead you to make decisions based on false conclusions, and those decisions don't just hurt you; they have the potential to hurt others.

So the next time you see two events occur in sequence, pause before you assume cause—because the moment you stop questioning that connection is the moment you start blaming roosters for the sunrise.

Chapter Nine

You're Never the Smartest One in the Room

I once asked a question in class that I thought was a good one. It was the kind of question I had asked many times before, and I was confident I knew exactly where it would lead. Hands went up. Answers came back. All of them were what I expected. Then one student raised a hand and gave an answer that didn't fit what I was expecting at all. At first, I thought the student had misunderstood the question. But when I asked him to explain his thinking, something unsettling and important happened. I realized the problem wasn't the answer. The problem was my question. The student had seen something I hadn't. That moment stayed with me, not because I was embarrassed or because the student was brilliant, but because it reminded me of something I had learned over time, the same quiet truth returning again and again: no matter how smart the person at the front of the room may be, there is always more intelligence sitting in the room than just their own.

That moment in the classroom showed that thinking improves when more than one mind is involved. A relative of mine told me about a study comparing how doctors explain medical information to patients and how artificial intelligence does the same. The researchers didn't just look at accuracy. They asked people to rate which explanation was clearer, more empathetic, and easier to understand. In those ratings, people consistently favored the AI explanations.

That might sound like a blow to the medical profession, but it actually isn't. What made the AI explanations so strong wasn't that they "out-thought" human doctors. Instead, every line of explanation they gave had been shaped by the insights, patterns, and communication styles of thousands of expert minds from all over the world. They didn't outthink them. They assembled them and then synthesized what they knew. When you bring that much human expertise together in one place, the result can be clearer and more helpful than what any one person might come up with alone.

Lehman College once reached out and offered to run a free course for my staff. It was a generous offer. Two professors would provide the instruction, and my teachers would participate. But something about it didn't sit right with me. I knew my staff. These were seasoned professionals, people who had spent years in real classrooms, dealing with real students and solving real problems every day. Their knowledge wasn't just book knowledge. It came from experience. And I didn't want this to turn into a situation where the professors did all the teaching and we just sat there taking notes. I wanted everyone in the room, my teachers and the professors alike, to be learners and contributors at the same time.

So I made a proposal: instead of a traditional class, why not create a classroom where both groups could teach and learn from each other? To their credit, the professors agreed. What followed was still a training session, but not the kind teachers had learned to expect. It dissolved the wall between teachers and professors. No one was there to perform or defend a title. Everyone took turns being the expert and the learner. The learning didn't just improve — it became something my staff didn't resent, because it finally respected what they already knew.

I remember another moment, from earlier in my career, when I was a middle school teacher. I gave my students an assignment built around a problem created by NASA. They were told their spaceship had crash-landed on the moon and that they had to decide what items would matter most for survival. Each student was asked to rank the items from most important to least important, based on how much each one would affect their chances of surviving, and then submit their answers. Afterward, the class was divided into small groups, and each group was given the assignment of agreeing on a single ranking from the same list.

What happened next amazed me. Students who had struggled on their own came alive in the group discussions. They debated, collaborated, and defended their ideas. And when they compared their group rankings to NASA's expert solution, they saw something remarkable: their collective answers were more accurate than any of their individual ones.

In the early 1980s, shortly after President Nixon opened diplomatic relations with China, a new restaurant opened in Manhattan not far from where I worked. It was owned and operated by recent immigrants who had lived most of their lives within traditional Chinese society, untouched by Western influence. One day, I sent back a plate of meat dumplings. I had intended to order vegetable dumplings instead. There was no complaint, just a polite request to switch. What struck me wasn't the food, but what happened next. The waiter didn't just turn around and handle it. He stopped. He spoke with two or three other staff members. They exchanged a few quiet words with one another. Then the waiter brought the plate back to the kitchen. At first, it seemed inefficient.

I later learned that in traditional Chinese society, decisions, especially ones that affect others, are often made collectively. The goal isn't speed. The goal is wisdom. The belief is that group input leads to a better result. What struck me about that moment wasn't just how different it was from what I was used to seeing in American restaurants, but how clearly it showed me the value a different society places on group thinking. It was the principle of collective intelligence in action, quiet, natural, and deeply understood.

No one of us is as smart as all of us. When people feel heard and their input genuinely shapes the outcome, something happens that no single voice can create. Decisions improve. Morale rises. People know they mattered. This isn't about being smart. It's about recognizing the intelligence already sitting around you.

So if you want to grow intellectually, personally, and professionally, don't chase the illusion of being the smartest person in the room. Be the one who listens deeply. Be the one who opens the door for others to speak. Be the one who understands that collective thinking isn't a threat to your intelligence, but a gift that expands it. Because every person you meet knows something you don't, and every moment you choose to learn from them, you become wiser.

The wisdom you need isn't inside your head. It lives in the space you create for others to speak. You're never the smartest one in the room — and that's exactly how it should be.

Section III

Why Smart People Stay Stuck

Chapter Ten

When Everyone Nods in Agreement

I was in my kitchen when my daughter, holding her two-month-old baby, walked past the microwave and noticed it was running. She moved away from it and told me microwave ovens are dangerous—that they leak radiation, destroy nutrients, and might even cause cancer. She added that her obstetrician had warned her to stay away from them during pregnancy for those same reasons.

My first reaction was skepticism. What she was saying didn't fit my understanding or experience, and it sounded like one of those claims that spreads easily because it feels scientific without actually being so.

But I didn't argue. When something doesn't sound right and I'm not fully certain of the facts, I've learned to pause. My daughter often comes to me for advice, and she knows I'm usually well informed—but she's also waiting for the day I'm wrong. That moment would give her proof that I don't always know what I'm talking about, and it would make it easier for her to dismiss me the next time. So I stayed quiet. If I was going to say anything, it had to be right.

I started looking things up, confident I'd quickly confirm what I already believed. Instead, I found myself unsettled. A simple search for "the dangers of microwave ovens" produced page after page of alarming claims. Radiation leaks. Lost nutrients. Cancer. The headlines were dramatic and absolute. What bothered me wasn't just the claims themselves—it was how many sources seemed to agree.

For a moment, that agreement began to shake my confidence. When many voices repeat the same thing with certainty, doubt can creep in even when your instincts tell you otherwise. But the uneasiness never went away. It didn't feel like I was being convinced; it felt like I was being pressured.

As I looked more closely, patterns began to appear. Many articles repeated the same claims using identical language, without quotation marks, as if the words themselves had been formally stated somewhere—even though I could find no original source for them. The repetition created the impression of authority where there was none.

As I followed the evidence further, that conclusion was reinforced. Many of the articles traced back to two names—Anthony Wayne and Lawrence Newell—and to an organization they were said to represent. I couldn't find any credible information showing that either the individuals or the organization existed, or ever had. There were also frequent references to Soviet-era studies from the 1950s, a period not exactly known for careful or trustworthy scientific work. And finally, much of the remaining research that was cited was extraordinarily flimsy—small sample sizes, no replication, no identifiable researchers—none of it qualifying as reliable evidence.

When I turned to sources with established credibility, the story changed completely. Consumer Reports clearly noted that microwave ovens are safe when used properly and that they can even preserve nutrients better than boiling. Louis Bloomfield, a physicist at the University of Virginia, put it simply: microwaves heat food by exciting water molecules. There's no mystery and no hidden danger—just heat delivered in a different way.

What mattered wasn't the microwave at all. The danger was the illusion of certainty created when many voices repeat the same unexamined claim.

This experience reminded me of something easy to forget. Doubt isn't weakness when it's followed by effort. It's a signal. When something doesn't sit right—especially when everyone else seems to agree—that's often the moment worth paying attention to.

It may sound like this story is about microwave ovens, but it isn't. It's about what happens when agreement replaces thinking. Nodding along feels safe. It keeps conversations smooth and avoids conflict. But that comfort comes at a price. When you stop questioning, you stop learning—and when curiosity disappears, truth usually follows.

The next time you find yourself surrounded by agreement, take it as a cue to slow down—and not to speak up. You don't have to argue, and you don't have to perform. Just look a little more closely. Check the sources. Follow the trail if there is one. Then decide for yourself.

Once you hand your judgment over to the crowd, you shouldn't be surprised when they start doing your thinking for you.

Chapter Eleven

Don't Learn from the Best

We live in a world that worships performance and credentials, but that doesn't mean the best performers make the best teachers. Performing and teaching are two completely different skills.

Top performers often step into teaching roles with little preparation in how to teach. They know how to perform the skill, but that doesn't automatically mean they know how to help someone else learn.

Here's what I mean. If I woke up tomorrow and announced that I was a brain surgeon without ever having attended medical school, you'd laugh. If I declared myself an attorney without ever having gone to law school, you'd laugh again. It would be just as ridiculous for me to claim I could teach music, tennis, cooking, photography, or woodworking without ever being trained to teach.

When people choose an instructor of any kind, they usually focus on how well that person performs in the field, not on the ability to teach — even though teaching skill is far more important, because the goal isn't to admire skill, it's to learn it.

Unfortunately, many people assume that excellence at performing automatically means excellence in teaching, but it doesn't. It's especially well illustrated in the dance world.

Most dance instructors were never trained to teach, or they received only a few hours of instruction — often from someone who also lacked formal training. They may be excellent dancers, but they don't always have the instructional knowledge that effective teaching requires.

Gifted students often survive poor instruction and later say the teacher was excellent, mistakenly believing their improvement came from quality teaching. Average and struggling learners aren't so lucky. They may gain some confidence and memorize a few steps, but they don't develop real lead-and-follow skills. They invest time and money and walk away thinking they failed — when in fact, they were victims of inadequate instruction.

Some keep dancing with limited skills, content enough to stay on the floor despite those limits. Others eventually quit. Years later, when asked whether they ever danced, they shrug and say, "I took lessons a long time ago, but I don't remember much." They blame themselves, never realizing they should have learned real, lasting skills — the kind you remember for a lifetime — if only they had received quality instruction.

In schools, the strongest math students are often chosen to help others — not because they were trained to teach, but simply because they can do the work.

Outside of school, families looking for tutors for their children often turn to tutoring agencies. Some of these agencies, unfortunately, choose tutors based solely on their mathematics skills. They may be engineers, science majors, even accountants — people with strong technical ability but no training in teaching whatsoever. Performance is only one of the two qualifications that should be required. The other is teaching ability, and that second qualification is routinely ignored.

So when a student still doesn't understand or doesn't perform well in mathematics after being tutored, it should surprise no one. The person responsible for their learning was never selected for the ability to teach, only for the ability to perform. Mathematics skill was mistaken for qualification to teach, and when that happens, responsibility for the failure rests far more with the absence of qualified instruction than with the student.

In many workplaces, the employee who knows the job best is often asked to train others. Sometimes it's a formal role for a week or two. Other times it's informal — helping a new hire "get up to speed" or acculturate into how the business really works.

While the selection of that person may seem logical, it is only the right choice if that person has some teaching training or at least considerable teaching ability. Doing the job and teaching someone how to do the job are not the same skill.

So before you hire, follow, or trust someone to teach you anything important, ask yourself one simple question: are you choosing them because they can do it, or because they can teach it?

In the end, what matters most is not what that person is able to do, but what he is able to teach you to do.

Chapter Twelve

Read Tomorrow's Newspaper Today

The chain was thin and hardly noticeable, the kind of thing most people would never see. I saw it immediately. It ran from a student's belt loop to his back pocket, and it wasn't being waved around or used to intimidate anyone. It was just there, doing what it was meant to do, keeping a wallet from being stolen. I knew why he wore it, and I had no doubt that he meant no harm. Still, I confiscated it.

He asked the same question I had heard many times before: "Why do you have to take it?" That is exactly the way they said it. I told them I trusted them — but I couldn't trust what might happen if the chain fell into the wrong hands. To you and me it might seem harmless at the moment, but it could become dangerous in somebody else's hands. I had to focus on that rather than on the innocent intentions of the student. Then, of course, the next question followed: "Can I get it back at the end of the day?"

I answered the same way every time. "Yes, but your mother will have to come and pick it up. It will be returned to her, and she will likely hand it right back to you." Most students accepted that, but every so often one would push just a little further and ask why he couldn't just come and pick it up himself.

That was when I would say the part that mattered most. I explained that if I gave the chain back to them and it was later used as a weapon anywhere, on the bus, in the hallway, or after school, I could already imagine the headline: *Stupid Assistant Principal Returns Dangerous Object, Student Injured.* I'm not going to let that story get written. I value my job.

Every student understood immediately. You could see it in their faces. They didn't accept the outcome because I was rough with them or threatening in any way. They accepted it because I was honest with them and took the time to explain the consequence I was trying to avoid. They knew I wasn't being arbitrary, and they knew I was thinking about what could happen for them as well as for me. That is my best example of the importance of reading tomorrow's newspaper today.

You've just seen this instinct at work. Now it's time to use it yourself.

It may sound clever at first, but it's really nothing more than a way to think before you decide. You don't analyze — you imagine. You picture the worst thing that could come out of what you're about to do. If what you see bothers you, you stop. And if you don't see anything unacceptable, you move ahead.

Sooner or later, every parent gets asked the same question. Your teenage daughter wants to go to a party. Before you answer, you stop and read tomorrow's newspaper today. You ask yourself, *what is the worst thing that could happen?* And you begin to picture it. A group of kids with no adult supervision. Alcohol being passed around. Underage drinking. The police showing up. Your child and others being questioned, maybe arrested, and you standing there trying to explain why you, as the adult, allowed this to happen.

That picture changes what you do next. You call the parent whose child is having the party to find out what the adult supervision really looks like and whether you approve of the people providing it. Maybe it even leads you to decide to be one of the adults who supervise. And sometimes, after thinking it through, it leads you to say no. When you explain why, your daughter may still be annoyed, but at least she understands that you weren't being arbitrary. You were trying to protect her.

You pull into a parking lot with your dog in the back seat, thinking you're just going to run into the store to grab a cup of coffee or pick up something quickly. You tell yourself you'll only be a minute. You've done this before and nothing happened, so it feels safe.

Then you read tomorrow's newspaper today. You picture yourself walking back to the car and seeing that the fire department has already arrived and is in the process of trying to rescue your dog from the rising heat inside your car. You imagine your dog panting and struggling to survive and a crowd gathering around. And finally, you envision yourself explaining to the police that you were only gone for a minute.

Because you read tomorrow's newspaper today, you didn't go into the store. Your dog remained safe, and you never had to read that newspaper article about you and your dog.

Some decisions are huge. Others feel so small that you don't even realize you're making a decision. But both have the potential to change your life. Before you make any decision, pause. Read tomorrow's newspaper today and picture what, if anything, could go wrong. And if you don't like that story, change what you're about to do.

It's definitely not about needing better instincts. It's about adopting one habit: envisioning the terrible or unacceptable thing that could happen before you act. Making that your standard way of thinking will save you from everyday decisions you would later regret, and from others you might otherwise spend the rest of your life wishing you could undo.

Chapter Thirteen
The Future Isn't Asking for Your Agreement

Everything around us is changing faster than ever — how we live, how we learn, how we talk to each other, how we work, even what we believe is possible. Yet people still act as if the world is supposed to wait until they feel ready. It won't.

The future isn't asking for your agreement. It's going to happen whether you like it or not. Writing petitions or begging for it not to happen is just another way of avoiding reality. It doesn't knock politely or wait for permission. It moves forward whether invited or not, and the people who make it through that kind of storm aren't the ones who fight it. They're the ones who stay curious, ask questions, and make what's new part of their lives.

The music industry learned this the hard way. When I was a kid, records spun at 78 revolutions per minute — thick, heavy discs that broke easily. Then came the 33s, long-playing albums that could hold a dozen songs, followed by the smaller 45s with one song on each side. That was evolution — slow, steady, and natural. By the time I was a teenager, vinyl was replaced by tape, and as a young adult, tape gave way to CDs. Each step felt like progress until digital file sharing arrived.

This time the industry didn't see evolution. They saw a threat to control and profit and prepared to defend what they already had. They called it theft, labeled it immoral, and threatened lawsuits, but the change went on without them. The model eventually shifted anyway. Musicians stopped relying on CD sales and began earning their livings through concerts, branding, social media, and fan support, while the companies that waited too long didn't disappear because they were wrong — they disappeared because they refused to move.

Other industries noticed what was coming sooner. When the public turned against cigarette smoking, tobacco companies didn't argue with the trend. They diversified, invested elsewhere, and adjusted their business models. Some survived. It wasn't that they were nicer people or suddenly cared more. It was that they finally realized that fighting the change wouldn't help them — the time had come to change their approach.

The publishing industry is facing the same problem right now. Artificial intelligence is already woven into daily professional work in medicine, law, education, research, and business, and writers use it to draft, revise, organize, and test language. But many publishers are reacting by simply refusing to look at any book that used AI in any way, as if that could undo what has already changed. Tools don't replace writers — they never have. Word processors didn't remove the need to think. Search engines didn't remove the need to judge. Spell-check didn't remove the need to choose words. Each of them simply shifted where effort was spent.

In the mid-1980s, as word processors began replacing typewriters, I attended a workshop for heads of English departments. A journalist described the divide in his newsroom: some reporters had made the switch, others insisted on staying with their machines. The ones who had switched said they'd never go back. The rest were convinced nothing important had changed, and within a few years, no one was hiring people who refused to work digitally.

When routines are disturbed, some people don't just feel inconvenienced — they feel lost. In earlier generations, change often arrived slowly enough that a person might be faced with only one or two major shifts in a lifetime. Today it arrives in waves, each one unsettling the ground beneath us that we thought was solid. Many respond by resisting the change around them, but that only widens the gap between their world and the one they're actually living in.

Cursive writing is a small but very revealing example. It stirs strong emotions among adults, and many defend it out of nostalgia. But let's be honest about how the next generation actually lives. They don't write essays by hand — they type them. They text on their phones, collaborate online, and submit most of their academic work electronically. Many don't even carry pens to school anymore; they go virtually unused. Students have computers at school. When adults buy a house, sign contracts, or fill out medical forms, it's all done digitally — and if someone still wants to sign in script, they can do that electronically through tools like DocuSign. The world no longer runs on cursive writing, and in the coming years it will be nearly extinct.

The future isn't asking for your agreement, so the question isn't how to stop change or bring the past back — it's whether you're going to build a small, comfortable world that's out of step with everything around you, or stay curious, keep learning, and use change to make your life richer instead of smaller.

Chapter Fourteen

What's Stopping You?

Dancers are some of the most dedicated people I know. Dancing isn't just an interest, it's a passion. They spend years sharpening their skills, take class after class, practice endlessly, and drive long distances just to be on the right floor with the right music. So you would think nothing could stop them. Right?

And yet, give some of them a little rain, just a little, and suddenly they've got the excuse they were waiting for. The rain isn't the issue. It simply gave them permission to do what they unknowingly wanted to do anyway.

I live in Florida, where it can rain two or three times a day. Many of us own umbrellas and rain gear. We move from our houses to our cars and from our cars to covered entrances. We know rain is just water. Even so, give some people a few sprinkles and somehow it becomes the excuse they're looking for not to go somewhere. Sometimes it really is about safety or sound judgment. But more often, people are simply looking for permission to stay home and remain comfortable. And once they find even the smallest excuse, no matter how irrational, it feels like relief, like a justification that lets them off the hook.

In schools across the country, teacher training often takes place on what become half days for students. To create that time without forcing teachers to stay after their regular hours, schools shorten each instructional period slightly. Students still attend every class, just in a condensed format, and all those trimmed minutes add up to the professional training time educators need. A half day makes school easier for kids. The day is shorter, the emotional pressure is less, and they get to come home earlier than usual. But that's not how students experience it. To them, a half day makes attendance feel optional, and as a result a high percentage choose not to come to school at all. It provides them with the very excuse they were looking for not to show up. Adults aren't any different. When people hear "optional," it quietly starts to translate to "don't bother" unless the experience promises to be spectacular. That's the excuse that wears the mask of "optional."

Just as kids give themselves permission to walk away from the responsibility of attending school because it's only a half day, adults do the same thing with their New Year's resolutions. You hear it when someone says, "Last year I committed to starting a diet on Monday, and by Tuesday I had already failed. So why bother making a New Year's resolution again this year?" That past failure provides permission to avoid trying again or making a serious commitment to change. The details change with age, but the habit is the same — using an excuse to avoid responsibility.

Somebody hears about a class or a dance and says, "They're having another one next week. I'll just go then." But when next week comes, they still haven't gone. The same thing happens when someone is thinking about going to the gym. "I'll go later, it's open until eight." And eight o'clock comes and goes, and they still haven't left. When people believe something will always be available, some quietly treat the present moment as optional. That's what I call the excuse that wears the mask of "later."

This chapter isn't called *What's Stopping Everybody Else*. It's called *What's Stopping You*. And the truth, the part most people don't like to admit, is that what's stopping you is often you. If you give people any excuse not to do something, most will take it—not because the excuse is logical, but because it makes things easier. It lets you stay comfortable. People aren't held back nearly as much by circumstances as they are by the excuses they create for themselves.

When people give themselves reasons for not doing something, those reasons usually sound logical and feel responsible. But sometimes they aren't guidance at all — they're just excuses dressed up to look like reasons so you can avoid doing something. That's the moment you have to stop and pay attention. If those reasons are genuine, then follow them. If they aren't, they're just excuses that you have to refuse to accept. Because every time you let excuses masquerade as reasons, it isn't circumstances that stop you — it's you.

Chapter Fifteen

You're Not Stuck—You're Just Thinking Like Everybody Else

I was the only Bronx boy walking into a cowboy party. The school secretaries in our district had their own social group, and one month they invited all the school-level administrators to a themed night in our honor. The theme was simple: Boots, Hats, and All Things Cowboy.

Most of the administrators were comfortable with that world. This was Florida, and many had Southern or Western roots, so cowboy boots and hats weren't new to them. But that image didn't come naturally to me, so I decided to have some fun with it. I went as the New York cowboy, dressed head-to-toe in black, boots, pants, shirt, bolo tie, and cowboy hat. I wasn't aiming for Texas. I was aiming for New York City.

The event hadn't even started when Al, a close friend of mine and an assistant principal at our school, realized he had left his cowboy hat in the registrar's office. He had the rest of his outfit, but the hat mattered. It was a full ten-gallon hat, the kind that makes the whole costume. Without it, he looked half-dressed. Unfortunately, it was locked in the office and, given the late hour, no one present had a key.

Most people would have said, "Forget it. You'll have to go without." That's reasonable, and that's normal. That's what almost everyone else would have done. But that's not what we did. We went to the registrar's office to see what options we had.

When we reached the registrar's office, we could see straight inside through the large interior window. And there, plain as day, was Al's ten-gallon hat sitting on the data-entry clerk's desk. The window wasn't the kind that opened. It was a solid pane, likely shatterproof Lexan or maybe even bulletproof glass. In the center was a round hole about five inches across, meant only for someone in the hallway to speak to the registrar. That was it. No access. Al looked at me and said, with total certainty,

"There's no way we can get in." I didn't agree with that conclusion. I looked at him and said, "Yes, we can."

We left the office and headed for the golf cart we used to get around our very large campus. Since I had already told Al, "Yes, we can," he looked at me and said, "But we only have fifteen minutes." I answered, "Well, given that short amount of time, you're asking the impossible." And that was that — or so it seemed.

We had barely driven off when something in me refused to let it go. As we passed the next building, I saw straight through the glass doors into a renovation area and spotted a stack of long metal rods, ceiling suspension tracks used to hang acoustical tile. I yelled, "Stop the cart." Even though we were moving at a reasonable speed, the large glass doors let me spot a perfectly placed pile of construction materials inside, long metal rods stacked in the middle of it all. They were about eighteen feet long, narrow, and extremely sturdy, and in the blink of an eye the whole plan snapped into place. I jumped off the cart, and before Al could say a single word, I had already entered the building, grabbed one of the eighteen-foot poles, run back out, and with the pole in my hand jumped onto the cart and told Al to drive us back to the registrar's office. He was so taken aback by how fast it happened that he just stared at me, frozen like a deer in headlights. He didn't say a word. He just followed my command.

Back at the registrar's office, which sat inside a larger administrative suite, I walked into the outer office. Our school resource officer, who was conducting a meeting there, paused, looked up, and watched as I entered dressed completely in black and heading straight toward the window in the registrar's office with an eighteen-foot pole in my hand. He didn't say a word.

I already knew about the locked window on the left-side wall and that it opened to the outside of the building. I stood in front of the thick glass panel and slipped the end of the rod through the circular opening. From where I stood, I could see the window lock clearly. Using the rod, I carefully worked the latch until it released. Then I pulled the rod back out and ran straight out of the office, past the school resource officer. Outside, I made my way to the now-unlocked window. I opened it, climbed inside, retrieved the ten-gallon hat, closed the window behind me, and exited through the front door, which locked automatically when I pulled it shut.

By the next morning, people were telling me that the school resource officer had spread the word. "Mr. Valerio came in last night dressed like Antonio Banderas from Zorro and burglarized the registrar's office." It gave everyone a good laugh, including me. And it said a lot about how quickly people walk away when the obvious way is blocked, locked door, no key, case closed. A locked door isn't the end. It's the beginning of a challenge. If there's no key, find a window. If there's no window, build a tunnel. If there's no tunnel, make your own door.

I served as assistant principal of a high school whose campus layout made very little sense. The original building had been constructed in the 1960s, and over the years the campus grew by altering that structure and adding new buildings wherever space allowed instead of following a master plan. The result was a maze of mismatched additions that was functional in places but disorganized as a whole.

One of the problems was that room numbers were not sequential. Room 30 was directly across the hall from room 101. Worse, the numbering system told you nothing about where a room was located. The number didn't tell you which building you were in, whether you were on the north or south side, or whether you were upstairs or downstairs. The only way to navigate the campus was to have the entire layout memorized, and that took a year or two.

I asked why no one had ever fixed it. The answer was always the same. Everyone had tried. Administrators, district officials, even outside consultants, and everyone hit the same dead end. The state controlled the official room numbers, and nothing could be changed without a full-campus reset and formal approval. Proposals were submitted. Requests were made. Nothing happened.

Since everyone who had tried and failed had gone through the front door — followed the rules, waited for permission, and failed, the challenge now was to examine the situation differently and create a way in that didn't exist yet.

So if we couldn't change the official room numbers, then we would have to keep them. However, that didn't prevent us from adding numbers that would actually serve the school's needs. I created a dual numbering system, one to satisfy the state and one to satisfy the school, and put them side by side on every door, with the school's number first.

For the first time, people could actually find their way around. The building code pointed them in the right direction, and the room numbers finally made sense. Kids weren't wandering the halls. New teachers weren't getting lost. And in one week, a problem that had been driving everyone crazy for decades simply disappeared, not because anything was forced, but because the situation was finally being looked at differently.

My phone had an issue that required a complete reset back to factory-new condition, and I had no idea how to fix it. So I used ChatGPT, an online artificial-intelligence tool, to walk me through the process. To my relief, I recovered nearly everything, contacts, photos, most apps. But I could not download Waze, which is my travel navigation app of choice. No matter what I tried with ChatGPT, Waze simply would not download.

Eventually, Chat suggested I try two other apps and told me the problem likely couldn't be solved from my end. In short, it threw up its hands and left me with a dead end.

That dead end became fuel. Instead of asking how to download Waze, I asked what was actually at the center of the problem. What was stopping the download in the first place? When Chat pointed to my Apple ID as the likely source, a clear path appeared. I created a second Apple ID, downloaded Waze, then switched back to my original one. Once the app was in place, it stayed there, fully functional and exactly what I needed. Just a change in how the problem was approached.

Most dead ends are not the final word. They only look that way when others have failed or concluded that it can't be done.

When you are facing an apparent dead end that has already stopped others, take that as the green light to start thinking differently. If you believe you are stuck, begin by assuming that you're not — you're just thinking like everybody else, and then change the way you examine the problem until a new path appears.

Section IV

How Influence Really Works

Chapter Sixteen

Stop Telling—Do This Instead

I've spent years sitting in classrooms watching teachers do what they and the rest of us often get wrong. A grammar lesson begins with the difference between *to*, *two*, and *too*. Then it moves on to *there*, *their*, and *they're*. The kids nod, the teacher relaxes, and a few answer correctly. From the front of the room, it looks like understanding.

The next day the teacher gives a test and the papers come back with high grades. Everything looks successful until the teacher reads the compositions. That's when the truth shows up. Students are still using *to* when they mean *too*. They're still confusing *there*, *their*, and *they're*. The answers were memorized, but the learning never showed up.

That moment doesn't belong only to teachers. We all live it in one form or another. We hear someone repeat our words and we walk away thinking we've helped, when all we've really heard is a borrowed answer. Telling is very good at creating recall and incredibly poor at creating understanding.

Knowledge that's told to us never really feels like our own. Our understanding is stronger and our ability to recall is better when we discover something ourselves, often through conversation and observation. When we're asked into knowledge rather than instructed, we build it our own way, we take ownership of it, and it stays with us.

The next time someone asks you a question, don't answer it. Pause. Ask one question back instead, not to test that person, but to help him uncover the answer for himself. Sometimes it takes one question. Sometimes it takes a short series of them. The goal is simple: ask in a way that helps people reveal what they already know and discover what they don't. That's when learning becomes theirs.

Early in my career, I remember a particular day when a student asked a simple question and I answered it immediately, without pausing, without asking anything back. It was pure reflex. The next day, during a discussion, he said something that made it clear to me that he had memorized my words but never truly understood them.

Then it struck me, he could repeat my words, but he didn't understand what they meant. My answer had given him information, not insight. So I tried something different: a series of logical, step-by-step questions to help him connect the dots and see how each idea led naturally to the next. When he finally reached genuine understanding, I saw it in his face. He hadn't been given the answer, he had built it himself. In that moment, I realized I wasn't witnessing comprehension, I was witnessing ownership. And that changed everything I thought I knew about how people learn best.

Once I stopped trying to be the source of every answer, my role changed. I wasn't there to give knowledge, I was there to draw it out. That shift worked in classrooms, in family interactions, with friends, and everywhere else in my life. It became clear that the questions I asked mattered far more than any answers I could give. When people build ideas for themselves, they remember them. That process sharpens how they think, how they reason, and how they reach conclusions, and over time those ideas become part of who they are.

You don't need more explanation here. You already know this works, because you've felt it again and again throughout your life. You've felt the difference between being told what to think and being helped through the process of thinking your way to your own conclusions. What you were told is often forgotten. What you discovered with the help of someone who questioned you has stayed with you over time.

So the next time you feel the urge to answer, stop and do what you already know is right. Think about the question you're going to ask, listen to the response, and ask another question. Keep going until you've helped others think it through and reach strong conclusions on their own.

Don't make people dependent on you. Every time you rush to answer, you teach them to parrot your words instead of thinking for themselves. You make them more dependent on you and less on themselves.

When you pause and ask instead, you aren't just helping people get answers. You're helping them build real knowledge, think more clearly, and grow more capable and confident.

There is no more effective way to help other human beings learn.

Chapter Seventeen

Stop Expecting People to Do What They're Supposed to Do

It's fine to expect some people, some of the time, to do what they're supposed to do. But expecting everyone to follow through every time is wishful thinking — and it doesn't work.

Expecting others to follow through without ever checking on their progress is almost a plan for failure. And this isn't just about bosses or employees — it's about parents, teachers, managers, friends, even consumers. In every part of life where we count on others to do what they've said or what's expected of them, we can't just assume. We have to make sure.

Some time ago, my nineteen-year-old son returned home, re-enrolled in college, and started searching for a part-time job. I was thrilled and wanted to help. We talked about applications, résumés, and preparing for interviews. But after months of trying, he still hadn't received a single call, so I asked to see one of his applications.

That's when everything became clear. It wasn't that he lacked experience or potential. The problem was the way he answered the questions. His responses raised red flags the moment I read them. The problem wasn't him — it was me. I had assumed that because we talked about how to fill out applications, he had learned it. But talking isn't teaching, and expectation isn't guidance.

I didn't criticize what he had written. Instead, I asked him, "What message do you think an employer gets from saying you left your last job because of a disagreement with a coworker?" That one question changed everything. He revised his application, and more importantly, he walked away having learned a crucial lesson.

For years as a teacher, I had understood this concept, but that experience with my son helped me realize it applied to parenting too. And when

I became principal, I saw that it applied to leadership just as well. The truth is, it applies to anyone trying to help others learn, grow, or succeed.

I used to tell people who wanted to become school administrators that I could summarize a thirty-credit master's course in one sentence: "They sometimes do what the principal expects, but they always do what the principal inspects."

Now, I know the word *inspect* can sound formal or even intimidating. But in practice, it was never about strict oversight or control. It was about guidance and support. Inspection, the way I did it, was simply following up to help people succeed.

When I met with staff, we talked about what they planned to accomplish and when. Together, we outlined the key steps and agreed on realistic dates for each one. I built those checkpoints into a shared calendar so timelines were visible and easy to follow. My secretary often called the person responsible ahead of time — not as a warning, but as a courtesy — to ask how things were going and whether they needed anything before I met with them.

The results spoke for themselves. Communication improved. Work moved forward. People felt supported because they knew someone cared enough to check in — not to find fault, but to help them finish well.

The real purpose of inspection isn't control — it's compassion. The best and most human thing we can do is to offer support when we have any reason to believe that someone will do better with help than when left entirely on their own. Following up isn't doubting their ability — it's caring about their success.

The same logic applied in the classroom. Highly effective teachers don't just assign a term paper and wait. They establish checkpoints — topic approval, thesis check, first paragraph — each one designed to prevent small issues from becoming big ones. That's not micromanagement. That's leadership.

Expecting someone to do something in its totality is sometimes not enough. It often relies more on hope than on sound understanding. Expectation, when combined with supportive inspection, becomes something entirely different. That's structure. That's guidance. That's genuine support.

When you have expectations of people, that sometimes isn't enough

— not in parenting, not in leadership, not as a consumer, not anywhere. If you want people to be successful — if you want real results — you can't just expect; you have to inspect. Of course, that doesn't mean inspecting everything or everyone. Some people — and some tasks — don't require it.

The moment you feel that someone is not going to follow through, your alarm system is already going off. And warnings like that can't be ignored.

Chapter Eighteen

The Most Loving Thing You Can Do

Most parents say they believe in rules, responsibility, and consequences, especially when the story is about someone else's child.

Then one day their own child is sitting across from them in a school office, facing a real consequence, and something shifts. The rules don't feel abstract anymore. The belief that discipline matters is suddenly competing with a powerful instinct to protect.

In school administration, I saw the same pattern over and over. A child makes a mistake and an adult steps in to correct it. The child comes to understand what went wrong, learns the lesson, and grows from it. But too many parents interrupt that pattern by rushing in to rescue their child, and the very process that was supposed to make the child stronger never gets to happen.

Parents don't make life easier when they rescue their child from consequences. They make life harder, because rescue replaces reality with protection and leaves that child unprepared for a world that is tougher and far less forgiving. If we want our children to become strong, confident, capable, independent adults, we have to stop rescuing them from reality.

Schools exist to prepare children for the real world, not to replace it with a safer one, and this is where so many parents get it wrong. They believe the school is punishing their child. Schools are not trying to punish children. Punishment is retribution. It says, "You did something wrong, so now I'm going to hurt you back." It's ugly, it's emotional, and it has no place in a child's life. That is not what schools are trying to teach.

A consequence is something completely different. It's natural. It's how the world works. A consequence says, "You made a choice, and this is what follows from that choice." Consequences aren't revenge. They're the natural, expected outcome of poor choices. They are reality, and reality is where the best learning happens, period.

This isn't just about school. The same logic shows up in everyday places where almost no one successfully argues about the consequence. Take the late fee charged when you don't pay your rent or mortgage on time. That isn't punishment or retribution. It's the natural result of a choice you made, and it teaches you to pay on time. Choices matter, and the results of those choices are what help a person grow.

The same choice-and-consequence pattern shows up clearly in adult life. When an employee keeps showing up late or missing deadlines, upper management may decide a consequence is necessary. A strong supervisor doesn't undermine that decision or attempt to rescue the employee from it. He stands with management, backs the consequence, and makes sure the message is clear: not to hurt the employee, but to help that person grow into someone reliable, capable, and responsible. That agreement isn't punishment. It's helping the employee face the real world the way it actually works.

People repeat the same bad advice over and over again. They say, "Don't be your child's friend." They've got it all wrong. You're supposed to be your child's best friend all the time, from the day they're born, without fail, and throughout their lives. But you can't be the kind of friend who protects them from reality and still call yourself their friend. If you really want to be their friend, you have to part company for a few minutes when discipline is necessary. Because discipline, allowing them to receive the consequences of their actions, is what a loving parent does. It's not punishment. It's a parent caring enough to let a person grow.

More than once, my adult children came to me for financial help. I didn't hand out gifts. I offered interest-free loans, because even adults need consequences that belong to them. Repayment was the consequence, and it mattered. But when they were standing up to the real world, paying back what they owed with consistency and discipline, I often canceled the debt, not as charity or pity, but as recognition and reward for responsibility. They become legal adults, but a parent's responsibility doesn't disappear. It just takes a different form. I didn't impose consequences anymore. I let life do that the way it always does. But I stayed as their steady voice, their friend, and their loving parent, the one they could lean on when the real world was doing the teaching.

Good parenting isn't cushioning every blow. It's refusing to trade comfort now for weakness later. Real love doesn't protect children from consequences. Real love prepares people to stand tall in a world that won't cushion anything. The most important thing you can do is let your children, young or adult, face what belongs to them and stand right beside them while they do.

It's a commitment you make to your children, young or adult, and to yourself, and it isn't something you half-do. When a moment comes that would normally make you feel the urge to step in and fix things for them, you stop instead, step back, and let the consequence stand. You do it every time, not occasionally, because inconsistency is a plan for failure. Every rescue weakens your child. Every time you hold the line with calm, steady love, you give children the strength to stand on their own. This is not a technique. It's a line you draw. And it may be the most loving one you will ever make.

Chapter Nineteen

How to Push a Mule Up a Hill

It's not always easy to get someone to do something you need or want that person to do. Sometimes it feels like you're dealing with a mule, stubborn, dug in, and not genuinely interested in what you're asking. Once we recognize that, most of us start pushing harder. We raise our voices, lecture, threaten, demand, and pressure in every way we know how. Some of us even take out a blowtorch and try to light a massive fire under them. And yes, sometimes that pressure gets a little movement. But more often it creates resistance, resentment, and outright unwillingness. Worse yet, it wears you down. You get frustrated, drained, and finally reach the point where it feels like it's time to stop trying. Every parent knows this cycle, repeating the same direction until the battle escalates and exhaustion takes over.

But there's a better way—a quieter, more effective method of getting people to do what needs to be done—and it doesn't require force, pressure, or frustration. Once you learn it, you'll wonder why you ever tried anything else.

The best way to move a stubborn mule—and life is full of them—is not with rage, but with a small, steady flame. Not hot enough to burn. Just hot enough to make standing still feel like the worst option.

Recently, as Vice President of our USA Dance Chapter, I needed our treasurer to authorize us to accept credit card payments. The president and I had worked out the process, but we were stuck without his participation. We decided to send him an email explaining the entire process, the legality of that process and why it made sense, telling him that we had already agreed upon doing this and that we wanted his input. Instead of responding, he sat on it for several days and did nothing.

The president and I discussed the lack of response and quickly realized we were dealing with a mule. We would have to encourage him rather than hit him with the blowtorch. We decided to contact the national USA Dance treasurer to confirm that our plan to accept credit cards was valid and in compliance with national policy. She confirmed that it was both legal and proper, so we shared her written statements with our treasurer in hopes that it would move him to action.

Our treasurer responded with an email showing that he agreed with the national treasurer's opinion. That was the purpose of going to her in the first place—to remove pressure from him and make moving forward easier. But he still took no action.

We wanted to move forward, but we decided to wait until after the first dance. We knew that his inaction would mean people who wanted to sign up that evening and become members would be unable to do so because we couldn't take their credit cards. And that is exactly what happened. Once that became a reality, we contacted him again in writing to explain that we lost membership as a direct result of his inaction. We believed that showing him the consequences would move him. And we were right, at least in terms of his acknowledgment. He agreed that it needed to be addressed and said he would take care of it.

But I still didn't know whether anything had changed. So days later, I contacted him through an email, asking what progress he had made. He apologized, said he had been extremely busy, and promised to make it a priority.

So I stayed on him, checking in again after the weekend and letting my actions make it clear that this was not going to fade away. After weeks of this, I finally asked him to get on the phone with me and Square so we could finish the process together.

He chose Monday at 9 a.m. We made the call. I sat at my computer and completed every step based on the information he provided and the directions given by the people from Square. Within an hour, the deed was accomplished. We had the ability to take credit cards.

It wasn't anger that got the job done, nor was it desperation. It was steady, calm, never-ending nudging—a flame that never burned anyone, but one that was never extinguished.

When I was a high school principal, I supervised an experienced, tenured teacher who had been permanently transferred to my school. His pedagogy was extremely weak, and he was someone most seasoned professionals in my field would consider untouchable, because he had both tenure and many years of satisfactory service. So I planned to let the process itself do the work.

I planned to follow the same professional process I would use with any teacher who was new to my school or showed signs of weakness. That meant a series of unannounced observations across the semester—each followed by specific recommendations, and later, a return visit to see whether those recommendations had been implemented. In most cases, that kind of structured professional development would strengthen a teacher. But in his case, I already knew that improvement wasn't likely. I had observed enough to see that the problem wasn't technique—it was who he was in the classroom. Visit after visit, feedback after feedback, the heat would quietly stay on, applying appropriate pressure without unfairness, confrontation, or hostility.

However, even the best plans can run straight into resistance. On the first unannounced observation day, he was absent, so I simply rescheduled. On the second unannounced visit, he was absent again. When I returned to my office, I vented my frustration to my secretary about not understanding how he always seemed to anticipate my visits. That's when it clicked. While she was out of the room, he was likely accessing my appointment book and seeing the days I planned to observe him. These repeated absences made it clear that he was avoiding observation. That's when I devised a method that made absenting himself ineffective.

I began writing "Observe Mr. Callahan (name changed to protect privacy)" on every school day in my appointment book for the rest of the year. Then I placed a small dot inside the "O" in "Observe" to indicate the actual days I intended to observe him. Only my secretary and I knew what the dot meant. And I asked her to continue her usual practice of retreating into the bathroom whenever he arrived, giving him full access to the appointment book and allowing him to see that he was scheduled to be observed every single day. In doing so, he no longer had the comfort of believing that absence could protect him. Instead of waiting for an occasional unannounced visit, he now believed that any day could be the day, and that uncertainty did the work quietly and effectively. By the end of the semester, the silent pressure had built high enough within him that he voluntarily requested a transfer.

Other situations call for a different version of the same flame—not one built on discomfort, but on encouragement. As assistant principal in charge of an English department, I supervised one of my subordinates who was a tenured teacher with an excellent professional record. She was extremely knowledgeable and close to retirement. But occasionally she engaged in conduct that was both illegal and, in my opinion, educational malpractice. She had trained her students to recognize a signal: a picture of a bird taped in the window of her classroom door meant that she would not be present for the last period of the day, and the students were free to go home. It was illegal because she was being paid for work she did not do, and irresponsible because students have an absolute right to a full instructional period every single day school is in session.

I didn't confront her directly or threaten her with charges. Given her tenure, her decades of strong performance, and her nearness to retirement, doing so would almost certainly have failed and created more problems than it solved, possibly even diminishing her performance for all of the other students she taught. Instead, I chose a different kind of flame—one built on encouragement. I regularly praised her writing, admired her speaking ability, complimented her television appearances, and talked about the possibility of her moving fully into that secondary career. By the end of the year, she voluntarily retired, and stepped into that next chapter with both dignity and purpose.

When you're dealing with someone unwilling, unmotivated, evasive, or stubborn, force usually makes things worse. The better move is to decide what kind of steady pressure will actually work for that person and then apply it quietly and consistently. No blowtorch, no threats, no drama. Over time, that steady pressure does the job. People either begin doing what they've been avoiding, or they reach the point where the discomfort becomes so great that they do whatever it takes to get out of it. Some comply. Others run. But no one stays dug in forever like a mule.

Section V

Recalibrating the Inner Scale

Chapter Twenty

You Hold the Scale

Life can get way too serious sometimes, and when too many moments of your day feel like that, it just gets heavier and heavier. Even Shakespeare understood that people need a break. In the middle of his darkest tragedies, he always paused to make you laugh—even if only for a moment. That wasn't an accident. It was intentional, because he knew people can only take so much. We need laughter in moments like that to restore balance—because without it, life becomes emotionally exhausting, and sooner or later it just wears you out.

The Jewish people—and I'm culturally one of them—have learned to laugh in the darkest of times. I once heard a Holocaust survivor say, "If we didn't laugh, we'd go crazy." You can see this kind of humor beautifully illustrated in *Fiddler on the Roof*. Tevye talks to God the way you'd talk to an old friend—honest, a little worn down, and quietly funny. "I know, I know—we're the chosen people. But once in a while, can't you choose someone else?"

No single culture invented the idea of balance. They just found different ways to express it. In Eastern philosophy, this idea is captured in the symbol of yin and yang—you've probably seen it before, a circle made of swirling black and white halves, each with a small dot of the opposite color inside. It isn't about choosing one side over the other. It's about understanding that the parts define each other, and that life only works when you adjust the weight you give to each piece instead of abandoning one altogether.

Sometimes life forces you to rebalance whether you're ready or not, but it still takes a moment of recognition before the rebalance can occur. My ex-wife's health no longer allows her to work a full-time job, and that limitation created more than one financial crisis. We had talked about flexible possibilities such as pet sitting and grocery shopping for the elderly—work that would let her control her own hours and pace. At some point, she began to face the truth that doing nothing wasn't just difficult—it was slowly closing every door she still had. Instead of letting that happen, she weighed what she could do against what she couldn't and then made a decision. By choosing a path that fit her limitations and still allowed her to earn, she created balance for herself. And while the hardship didn't disappear, it stopped being a problem with no solution.

Retirement is supposed to be your reward—the years when you finally have time to do the things you love. But it's also the stage of life when time no longer feels relatively unlimited. You begin to feel it closing in on you, and it changes how you see every day. I was DJing, building dance events, promoting them, serving as vice president of USA Dance, and spending time with my girlfriend going to museums, antiquing, and enjoying life. I was busy in all the right ways, and I loved that life.

Then one day I realized it would probably take me another year to finish my book, and that realization hit me hard. I didn't want to pass on without finishing that book—and the second one that was already forming in my mind and half-written. I was afraid I would miss the chance to do what mattered most to me in the time I had left. So I decided to accelerate the speed with which I was writing the first book while still continuing to work on the second. Without exception, I began writing every day as soon as I was up and settled in.

That's when the scale tipped. I was writing seven, eight, sometimes nine hours a day, getting up earlier and earlier, going to bed earlier and earlier, not shaving or showering until late in the afternoon. One night my girlfriend and I went to a dance in our community, and about ten minutes after we arrived she looked at me and said, "You're exhausted." She was right. She suggested I go home, and I did. The next morning, in consultation with her, I stopped, took several days off, and let the exhaustion lift. When I started again, I changed the rules. I now take care of myself first every morning—shower, shave, get dressed—and then I write, but only until the morning becomes afternoon. The afternoon has become protected territory, and slowly the old Jack has come back—the smiling, laughing, high-energy tornado and earthquake my girlfriend often calls me. Even my photographs show it. The happiness and balance have returned to my face. I didn't abandon my work. I finally learned how to add writing to my life without letting it take my life over.

The woman I love comes from Venezuela. She had once been at the top of her profession—trained in oncology and hematology, working in a hospital and running two clinics, financially secure, traveling the world, sending her children to schools in different countries. It was a life built carefully over decades.

That balance was destroyed by the governments of Hugo Chávez and Nicolás Maduro. Corruption hollowed out the economy, independent institutions collapsed, inflation exploded, hospitals ran out of medicine, and daily life became intolerable. Millions fled—not only laborers, but doctors, engineers, teachers, and other professionals who could no longer live or work in a society that was no longer productively functional. She was one of them, forced to abandon the life she had built.

She came to the United States hoping to regain stability, choosing this country because her daughter lived here and needed help caring for a child with a degenerative disease. For years she worked ten to twelve hours a day, seven days a week, devoting herself to that child so her daughter could survive. She earned citizenship, but lived almost entirely inside the home, with little exposure to American life and almost no opportunity to develop her English. The country had changed, but the imbalance remained—just in a different form.

At some point she recognized what was happening. She was safe, but she was no longer living her own life. Despite limited English, she found her own apartment, learned how to navigate social services, and created a modest but independent existence. She goes to the gym. She walks. She studies English. She dances at the community clubhouse on Saturday nights. Balance did not come from getting her old life back—it came from standing up and building a new one.

Look at the pattern here. In all three stories, the problem wasn't just hardship—it was imbalance. My ex-wife recognized that her limits were crushing her financially, so she weighed what she could do against what she couldn't and made a practical decision. I saw that my fear of unfinished purpose was draining the life out of me, so I changed how I structured my days. And the woman I love realized that safety without independence was still a life out of balance, so she stood up and built a new one from what she had left.

If something feels off or out of balance in your life, it probably is. And if you're waiting for someone else to fix it, don't hold your breath. You're the one holding the scale. If you know you're out of balance, it's up to you —and you alone—to bring yourself back into healthy balance.

Chapter Twenty-One

The Day You Put the Tools Away

Some people grow old by 30, not in their bodies, but in their minds. They stop changing, stop learning, stop seeing with curiosity and wonder. Once that mindset takes hold, it's nearly impossible to change. The body stays young and flexible, but the mind grows increasingly inflexible and resistant to change.

Others manage to stay youthful and vibrant well into their 80s, 90s, and beyond. People say it's unbelievable, but it isn't. It's not what you're born with or luck. It's simply what happens when you remain open to the world, when you keep learning, growing, and changing.

The real tragedy comes when people's openness closes and they begin planting the seeds of aging far too early in life. And once planted, they keep watering those seeds, nurturing them, feeding them, giving them everything they need to grow. But others never plant them at all. Or if a seed is dropped, they refuse to water it. They starve it and let it die. That's why some people remain alive in spirit, while others let their youth quietly slip away long before their bodies do.

Working with students meant constantly adjusting to who was coming through the door. Every few years, it was a new group—how they learned, what motivated them, what they valued, how they communicated. Because my job depended on reaching them, not changing with them wasn't an option. Five years later, it was different students with different expectations. That pattern repeated itself for 42 years. If I hadn't adapted, the disconnect between them and me would have grown wider. I would have become ineffective, unhappy in my work, and eventually burned out.

By the time many people reach their fifties or sixties, their daily world is made up almost entirely of people their own age. That's normal, but it often comes with a cost. Without consistent, meaningful exposure to the changes younger generations represent, it becomes increasingly easy to lose touch with the world as it evolves around us.

For some, that distance shows up as irritation with how things are done now. New ways of doing familiar tasks feel unnecessary or burdensome. Changes are met with criticism rather than curiosity, and the past starts to feel safer than the present. What you hear and see is discomfort with change, and beneath that, a wish that the world would slow down or return to what once felt familiar.

Cursive writing still stirs strong emotions among adults. Many cling to it out of nostalgia. But the reality is simple: today's kids don't use cursive, and they don't need to. Their communication is digital. They text on phones, write essays on laptops, and collaborate in cloud-based documents. Many don't even carry pens to school anymore. When you buy a house, sign a contract, or fill out medical forms, it's all electronic. And if you want, you can still sign in script. The world has moved on.

So why do people insist that schools devote precious time to teaching cursive? Because it feels familiar. Because it's what they learned. But schools today face serious challenges in literacy and numeracy. Every instructional minute matters. Spending months on a nearly obsolete skill to soothe nostalgia isn't just inefficient. It's misdirected.

In my 55+ community, when I ask for event information at the clubhouse, I'm told to "check Channel 63." Younger people wouldn't even know what a channel is. They don't watch broadcast television. They stream. I don't even have the equipment needed to watch cable or broadcast TV in my home. Instead, I stream news, shows, documentaries, and lectures on demand.

Not long ago, a visit to the doctor's office meant being handed a form and a pen. That still happens, but it's becoming increasingly less common. More often now, information is entered electronically on a tablet. When people in their sixties or older are handed a tablet, instructions are usually offered. They may be brief or detailed, but the offer itself is the point. It reflects long experience with patients in that age group who did not keep pace with the way everyday tasks are now handled. For that reason, assistance is commonly assumed. The same instructions are rarely offered to younger adults, because experience has shown they won't be needed.

When people resist learning, pull away from the young, and fear change, their world quietly shrinks. Younger generations are living windows into the future, but too often those windows go unnoticed. Instead, people cling to a past that no longer exists and miss the life still unfolding in front of them.

That's the key. Staying mentally young has nothing to do with creams, potions, or wishful thinking. It's about continuing to grow. The fountain of youth isn't something you find. It's something you practice.

Chapter Twenty-Two

Don't Let the Rain Blind You

Most people think they're seeing clearly when something bad happens. But when it rains in your life, when things go wrong, when trouble finds you, it's easy to become so focused on the rain that you lose sight of everything else in the sky. Rain doesn't just fall. It blinds you.

"Isn't this terrible?" I asked my son when I arrived at the scene of his car accident. I didn't really believe it was terrible. I said it to draw out how he was feeling because at his age and experience level, that's probably what it looked like. When he agreed, I shook my head. "No," I said. "It's not terrible at all. It's actually wonderful."

I wanted him to see a different perspective. He looked at me like I was crazy, but I pointed out a few things. "First, you weren't hurt. And no one else was either. That alone is reason to celebrate. Second, the car is going to be repaired, and since you were hit from behind, the other driver is responsible. His insurance will cover it. But more than that, you're going to have at least half the car repainted at no cost to you. And if we chip in a little more, you can have the whole car painted." You'll walk away with a car that looks brand new. You've always taken good care of it mechanically, and now it's going to look beautiful on the outside, too.

I was teaching in one of the roughest neighborhoods in the South Bronx, an area known at the time as Fort Apache. One afternoon I went out to my car, turned the key, and nothing happened. When I opened the hood, I saw that the battery was gone. The thieves hadn't cut the cables. They had loosened the bolts and taken it cleanly. It was getting late, the light was fading, and this wasn't a place you wanted to be after dark. After a few calls, a local mechanic lent me a battery so I could get home. The next day, on my way to replace it, I said to myself, "Jack, you have two choices. You can spend $200 on a new battery and be angry about it, or you can just spend $200 on a new battery." That was the moment I realized the real cost wasn't the battery.

One morning my wife and I were getting ready for work. She was substituting that day, running late, and I reluctantly agreed to wait so we could ride together. I sat in her car in the garage, getting more irritated by the minute. When she finally arrived, I backed out without looking and drove straight into my own car in the middle of the driveway. Two cars damaged. Two insurance deductibles. Five hundred dollars. On the way out she asked, "Aren't you going to get out and look at the damage?" I said, "No. I can get out, look at it, get angry, and still pay $500, or I can just pay $500 and not let it take over my day." I got out only because she insisted, then went to work. I wasn't willing to let it cost me anything more than money.

In the 1970s, getting a teaching job in New York City was nearly impossible. Thousands of men had entered the profession to avoid the draft during the Vietnam War, creating a massive surplus. I didn't even have a license, yet somehow I found my way in. I started teaching social studies and before long was teaching math and science at the same time.

Three years after entering the profession, I was granted tenure and handed a layoff letter at the same time. New York City was on the edge of bankruptcy, and layoffs began with untenured teachers. Because a much higher percentage of English teachers were untenured than in other subjects, English was hit far harder, creating unexpected vacancies. To fill them, the city issued provisional licenses to teachers who were close to completing the requirements. I was one of them.

What I didn't see then, but clearly see now, is that this constant instability was shaping how I would respond to uncertainty for the rest of my life. While it felt like one storm after another, I was learning not to let the rain blind me. In time I moved into school leadership, first as an assistant principal and later as a principal. The silver lining wasn't any single promotion. It was the movement through the storm that quietly trained me for leadership.

The next time something goes wrong, and it will, you may feel anger, disappointment, or frustration, or you may feel something else entirely.

What matters in that moment is asking yourself a simple question: Am I going to let this run my thinking, or am I going to decide where my attention belongs?

Chapter Twenty-Three

Why We Need to Understand People from Another Galaxy

People often say men are from Mars and women are from Venus. I disagree. Are you kidding? Those planets are practically neighbors, almost close enough to borrow sugar from each other. But men and women? It feels like we're from completely different galaxies. It took me years of wrong turns and unnecessary damage to understand just how far apart those galaxies really are.

When I was a young, inexperienced man, I remember picking up a woman for a date and pushing the car harder than I should have. I was turning corners without slowing down, weaving through traffic, and driving beyond the speed limit because I believed I was advertising something about myself. I didn't think I was being reckless. I thought I was showing coordination, confidence, and control, the way male birds jump and flip around to prove they're worth choosing. At least, that's what I thought I was doing.

But to her, what I was doing came across completely differently. Instead of impressing her, I was scaring the heck out of her and making her feel disrespected and unsafe. Fortunately, she recognized that I wasn't acting with bad intentions and calmly asked me to pull over so we could talk. "I wouldn't have gotten in the car with you if I didn't like and trust you," she said. Then she explained that she would feel far more respected, and far more impressed, if I drove carefully, like a gentleman who valued her safety and comfort.

For the remainder of the time we were together that day, I kept replaying what had happened, what she had said, and what that moment had revealed to me. I was beginning to see how two people could share the exact same moment and yet live inside completely different versions of it.

My mind even drifted back over the years before that day, making me wonder how many times I had believed that what I saw was the only version, when in fact a woman may have been seeing those moments very differently.

At first, I thought this disconnect belonged only to me, but I soon realized it was an issue for most men. Most of us were missing the same thing. We weren't recognizing that women could be living a very different experience from us, even in the same set of circumstances. And when I looked even closer, I saw that the misunderstanding was a two-way street. Women were misunderstanding men for the same reason men were misunderstanding women. We were sharing the same moments, but living them very differently.

Throughout my adult life, whenever one relationship ended and I began dating again, the cautions from female friends came fast and furious. I wasn't jumping into a new relationship, I was simply dating again, as I always had. Still, I kept hearing the same things: "You need time to heal," "You should take a break," "You need to find yourself before you jump into another relationship." Not one man ever said anything like that to me.

What struck me wasn't the concern, it was the misunderstanding behind it. The women in my life were offering me the same advice they would have given to their girlfriends without considering that I'm not a woman, I'm a man, and the way I and most men heal isn't the same as a woman does. We were looking at the same situation, but living it in a completely different way.

I often found myself facing the same gap when I was married to my second wife. She would come to me with something she was struggling with, and to me it felt obvious that she wanted a solution. So I offered one. When she didn't like it, I offered another. And before I knew it, I was proposing more solutions as she was pulling away from each. Eventually I'd get frustrated and say, "Well, if you don't want to hear what I think, then don't bother asking me for a solution!"

Then one day, in the middle of one of these exchanges, she suddenly exploded and yelled, "Don't you know that an emotional situation requires an emotional solution?" That line hit me like a house falling on my head. From that moment on, I began paying attention to her reaction to my first suggestion. If she rejected it, that became my cue to stop fixing and start listening. I learned to be present, to offer support instead of answers. Compared to the young man behind the wheel years earlier, I had come a long way, but I also knew I was still learning the language of another galaxy.

About six months ago, I began taking an interest in a woman who lives in my 55-plus community. We met for coffee, and what was meant to be brief turned into two and a half hours of easy, natural connection.

That same weekend we went to a dinner dance for our second date. During our conversations that evening, I sensed something I had learned about women over the years. She was the kind of woman who wanted to protect her privacy and keep a new relationship under wraps until she felt grounded and comfortable. She wasn't hiding anything. She was protecting her comfort and emotions until she was ready to share them.

Because we lived in the same community and both attended the same weekly dance, I knew that wouldn't be easy. Her friends were observant, and I had always treated her like a casual hello-and-goodbye acquaintance. Any change in that would be noticed immediately. That left me with a problem that didn't have a clear solution. If I became warmer in public, her friends might figure things out before she was ready. If I stayed distant, she might think I wasn't really interested. So I talked with her and asked how she wanted me to handle it. Her decision became my decision, because I finally understood I couldn't guess my way through this without risking mistakes.

She responded warmly. "Thank you again for understanding my concern." In that moment I realized something important. I hadn't guessed what was on her mind. I understood it. My actions reflected that understanding. None of it matched my natural instinct, but I was proud of myself. After many years, I had learned how to respect the needs of someone from another galaxy.

Once you understand that men and women don't react to the same situations in the same way, it becomes impossible to keep pretending they do. However, noticing that there is a difference is simply not enough. You have to start by asking yourself, "How is the other person actually experiencing this right now?" and then adjust how you respond, or you'll keep paying the same price.

When you finally stop expecting people from another galaxy to feel and respond the way you do, conversations become clearer, tension diminishes, and trust grows. Your relationships become more harmonious and more productive, and you begin to move through your life with far less friction and far more ease.

A Note To Readers

If this book meant something to you, I'd love to hear from you.

You can reach me at:
JackValerio.com

Afterword

I didn't write this book because I wanted to be an author.

I wrote it because I finally ran out of excuses not to.

For as long as I can remember, people have told me I should write a book. It happens whenever I help someone think through a problem or when a conversation turns into clarity. They say it casually, but they mean it. *You should write a book.*

People said that for years, and I never argued with them. I always agreed that I probably should, but I also told them just as plainly that I wasn't going to. I didn't go into detail. I usually brushed it off by saying I was lazy or that it was too much work.

That was the surface answer. What sat beneath it was something else. Writing a book is an overwhelming task, and I knew exactly what it would cost. It demands time, energy, and focus, and it disrupts your life in ways most people don't realize. Because I don't do anything halfway, I don't make commitments I'm not prepared to honor. When I make one like this, I have to be willing to give something up. I had responsibilities as a parent, a husband, a full-time educator, and more, and the question was always the same: Where does the time come from? What am I going to stop doing? For many years, my answer was no. Not because I couldn't do it, but because I understood exactly what it would cost.

I've always seen the world a little differently than the people around me. That doesn't mean I think I'm smarter or special. It simply means my mind works the way it works. I tend to look deeper than what's immediately visible. I pay attention to patterns, connect dots, and think carefully about consequences. That way of thinking has been part of me for as long as I can remember.

The ideas in this book didn't come from repeating what I was taught.

I learned from textbooks and from people who came before me, but I never stopped there. I expanded on what I was given and tested ideas against real life. I paid attention to what worked and what didn't. Over time, patterns emerged, and those patterns turned into principles I used to guide my own decisions and help others avoid mistakes I'd seen repeated again and again.

Many of the chapters began as a single sentence I heard somewhere along the way. I didn't always know what those sentences meant at the time. Sometimes it took years before their meaning became clear. I thought about them, tested them in real situations, and watched what happened when I acted on them. Over time, those fragments turned into principles I could live by. Other ideas didn't start with a sentence at all. They came from noticing something small that most people overlook, the way an artist notices negative space instead of the obvious subject. In every case, the ideas here didn't come from repetition. They came from conclusion, shaped by experience, trial and error, and a habit of looking at things from a different angle.

For most of my life, I shared those insights in conversations, in hallways, and in moments that mattered more than people realized at the time. Retirement didn't change that impulse. If anything, it freed it.

As I moved deeper into my golden years, time began to feel finite in a very real way, and it made me think more carefully about how I wanted to use it. I became more willing to try things, but also more willing to stop when something was no longer fun, when the effort began to outweigh the joy, or when it started to feel like an obligation. I wasn't trying to stay busy or fill time. I was looking for something meaningful enough to justify doing it.

Writing met every standard I had. It played to my strengths, demanded clarity, and gave me constant opportunities to learn and grow. More importantly, it became the way I could help others by sharing what I had to offer.

www.ingramcontent.com/pod-product-compliance
Lightning Source LLC
LaVergne TN
LVHW011048110826
845149LV00015B/3398

* 9 7 9 8 9 9 4 2 5 7 3 0 2 *